How to Line Up Your Fourth Putt

How to Line Up Your Fourth Putt

Bobby Rusher

DOUBLEDAY

NEW YORK   LONDON   TORONTO   SYDNEY   AUCKLAND

PUBLISHED BY DOUBLEDAY

Another edition of this book was originally published in 1990 by
Bogey Four Productions, a division of R. Paul Rusher & Co., Inc.
It is here reprinted by arrangement with R. Paul Runk.

Published in the United States by Doubleday, an imprint of
The Doubleday Broadway Publishing Group, a division of
Random House, Inc., New York.

www.doubleday.com

DOUBLEDAY and the portrayal of an anchor with a dolphin
are registered trademarks of Random House, Inc.

This book is totally fictitious, and all names, including
the author's, are figments. Any perceived similarity to real
persons, places, or circumstances is certainly coincidental.
Except for George, who is real, and who never broke 100 in his life,
no matter what he says. (See Chapter 29.)

Book design by Patrick Broderick/Rotodesign

Library of Congress Cataloging-in-Publication Data
Rusher, Bobby.
  How to line up your fourth putt / Bobby Rusher. — 1st Doubleday ed.
     p. cm.
  Originally published: Southport, Conn. : Bogey Four Productions, 1990.
  1. Golf—Humor. I. Title.
  PN6231.G68R88 2007
  818'.5402—dc22

                                                 2006010370

ISBN: 978-0-385-51895-6

PRINTED IN THE UNITED STATES OF AMERICA

This title may be purchased for business or promotional use or for
special sales. For information, please write to: Special Markets
Department, Random House, Inc., 1745 Broadway, MD 6-3,
New York, NY 10019 or specialmarkets@randomhouse.com.

10 9 8 7 6 5 4 3 2 1

First Doubleday Edition

This book was written for golfers who appreciate the simple pleasures of the strange trajectory and the mysterious bounce, and who can laugh at deep divots and the big banana.

CONTENTS

CONTENTS

CONTENTS

CONTENTS

On Announcing Your Handicap

As we all know, the handicap system allows the incompetent golfer to enjoy a round with a much better player.

It is of paramount importance to know how to handle yourself when queried about your "handicap." You must know how to mislead your opponent without feeling guilty because you lied. When someone asks, "Well, what's your handicap?" there are a number of things you can say:

1. You can tell the truth and say, "I'm a 36," and then proceed as usual to ruin what would otherwise have been a pleasant afternoon.

2. You can subtract thirty strokes from your actual handicap and announce you are a "6," but this is not a money-winning proposition, which is the whole point, right? Also, if you say

you're a "6" and are therefore paired
with a "24," your partner will put a
nine-iron to your *solar plexus* by the
third hole, because you are a Complete
Jerk. (See Chapter 13.)

3. You can add thirty strokes to your
   handicap, thereby leading to the
   embarrassing prospect of having to
   sheepishly grin and mumble, "I'm
   a 66." You don't want to do this either,
   unless you are a Complete Jerk. (See
   Chapter 13.)

4. Your best response is to repeat the old
   joke: "I usually shoot in the eighties;
   but if it gets any colder than that, I
   don't play at all." You will irritate a lot
   of serious golfers with this one, but,
   using techniques discussed later,
   you'll make money no matter what
   they think.

CHAPTER 1

How to Line Up Your Fourth Putt

OKAY. This method never fails. (Provided your third putt left you no more than six feet from the cup.)

1. Grab your putter.

2. Walk once slowly around the perimeter of the green mumbling the word "POO-POO-KAH-KAH" over and over, holding your club at arm's length in front of you. This is the beginning of the ceremony.

3. Stop and button your collar all the way to the neck.

4. Stand over the ball and look up at the sky. Raise your putter into the air with both hands and say, "This, by God, is it!"

5. Slowly look down at your ball. It will have moved to about two feet from the hole!

6. Remember all the things you have done wrong in life, keeping your chin on your breastplate.

7. Say "POO-POO-KAH-KAH" tightly one more time. Your ball will now be about one foot from the hole.

8. Step back, breathe deeply, and drop to your knees, "reading" the green intently. Quietly and gently say, "Aw, sheee...it."

9. Stand up! Throw your putter down and violently tear open the Velcro seal on your golf glove! Heave the glove into the nearest bunker. You will feel a serenity like none you've ever known.

10. Your ball will now be seven inches from the cup.

11. Now nestle that putter into your left hand, forming a "V" where your

thumb and index finger collide. Imagine a long, sharp stake running from the ball, through the clubhead, past the elbow, into the heart, and finally piercing the brain. That's it! This is the real beginning of the stroke itself, when ball, club, hands, heart, and brain are all connected by a long, sharp stake.

12. Cover your left hand by wrapping it with your right hand from the opposite side.

13. You should now be breathing heavily and whispering "POO-POO-KAH-KAH" softly but quickly. Your ball will be two inches from the cup.

14. Putt the damned thing in! If you miss, say "POO-POO-KAH-KAH" one more time.

CHAPTER **2**

How to Hit a Dunlop 2 from the Rough When You Hit a Titleist 1 from the Tee

TO ACCOMPLISH this without being penalized, you need Drop Pocket Golf Slacks.™ (See Chapter 10.) Basically, you feign an intense search for the lost Titleist, then drop the Dunlop silently using your new slacks. Simultaneously yell, "Found it!"

The key here is that you must be sure nobody knows what you actually hit off the tee. Be sure to tee your ball so that identifying marks, labels, numbers, and logos are all on the bottom of the ball.

CHAPTER **3**

When Trajectory Is Important on Short Putts

TRAJECTORY is important on short putts:

1. If you wish to enter the hole directly, without touching the rim of the cup at all, as in "slam dunk" or "swish" shots. (If you achieve this, please be sure to yell "SWISH," so your opponents know you meant it.) Your need to do this (to "slam dunk" a putt) can arise:

   A. When your opponent's ball is in front of yours

   B. When funds have been escrowed against the possibility of your actually executing the shot

   C. When you want to keep your balls absolutely clean

2. If the putt is over ninety yards long.

3. When you attempt to throw the ball into the cup, to preclude otherwise suicidal or homicidal behavior, because you lie eight on a par-three green.

CHAPTER 4

When to Chip from the Tee

WELL,

1. When you already lie six on that tee.

2. To demonstrate that your power and control are totally independent of the club you use.

3. To get back to the fairway (because to get to this tee, you sliced an approach to the third).

4. When you're playing with a Complete Jerk. (See Chapter 13.)

CHAPTER 5

The Art of Cleaning Your Balls When Your Opponent Is on the Tee

THIS IS is a great ploy, another certain moneymaker. Feign innocence and apology, but clean your ball loudly whenever you need to screw up your opponent's drive. He'll be upset, but most players won't go so far as to say anything; and for those who do comment, you can resort to alternative techniques described in other chapters. By the time most actually complain, they've already lost five strokes!

They'll get over it.

How to Avoid the Water When You Lie Eight in the Bunker

PICK UP.

How to Get More Distance Off the Shank

THIS CAN BE guaranteed by modifying your clubs the next time you have them re-gripped. Just ask your pro to attach two inches of grip material on the lowest part of the shaft, where shaft meets head, where ball meets shank. The hard rubber will double your normal shank yardage, known as "shankage."

CHAPTER **8**

How to Achieve the Flawless Swing Without Injuring Yourself or Loved Ones

THIS REQUIRES simple movements, the main goal of which is to avoid hurting your left leg or damaging your partner's forehead. The flawless swing is easy:

Make sure on the backswing that your armswing stretches the left half of your body around your right leg, which should be completely stationary at all times. If you are left-handed, insure that your rightswing pulls your backswing to the other side of your body, shifting one-third of your weight through the entire swing, until the end.

Otherwise, you'll miss the ball... or hurt somebody.

CHAPTER 9

Using Your Shadow on the Greens to Maximize Earnings

SHADOW PLAY is very, very effective on the greens, especially early in the morning or late in the afternoon, when long shadows allow you to interfere with your opponent's putting while still standing yards away, pretending to be polite. Even a slight movement at the proper moment can turn a birdie three into a bogey five. This technique was used to great advantage twice in the first round of the Seventh Bogey Fore Open. Those who were there still talk about it. Especially George, who never broke 100 in his life, no matter what he says.

CHAPTER 10

Where to Buy Pants with Drop Pockets™

MOST PEOPLE know about the special shoes and the unnecessary gloves in the game, but they do not normally become aware of the existence (and great utility) of other clothing until quite late in their careers.

My buddy Ernie was playing in '93 with a 36 handicap and was considered a valuable asset by his Partner. Partner was a good golfer, a serious golfer (a pain in the neck; see Chapter 13 on playing with a Complete Jerk).

One day, on the second hole, Ernie delivered a blow that sent his tee shot screeching low into the woods, far left, about 120 yards out. Partner screamed that they *had* to find that ball because Ernie got two strokes on the hole.

The foursome searched in vain, but Partner stayed behind to continue the search. When Ernie was about fifty yards away, Partner yelled that he had found the ball! Ernie couldn't believe

Hidden in glove is tiny remote-control device emitting a frequency which activates lever.

B. Lever releases balls one at a time. Aided by gravity, ball drops to ground.

C. Ball rolls to position.

it, but when he returned to the area, the ball was there, shining brilliantly in the sun, sitting softly atop a small mound of grass, in the middle of a dirt road. A clear shot to the green. Partner was truly pleased and grinned widely. Ernie whispered that he had hit a Titleist and that this was a Dunlop. Partner said, "Shut up and swing." So he did. Four net two. Great game, golf.

Partner later divulged the address of a store in Miami where Drop Pocket Golfing Slacks* are available.

---

* Send your pants and $100 to the author if you can't find a pair. Your slacks will be returned with pockets "dropped" and ready for score-lowering wear.

CHAPTER 11

How to Score Well at Night

NIGHTTIME GOLF is becoming very popular at certain clubs in New Jersey. Cooler, less crowded, and only slightly more dangerous for most players, successful play in the dark requires observance of just a few key rules:

1. You must wear your Drop Pocket Slacks (see Chapter 10) because they are most helpful at night (for obvious reasons).

2. Bring a kazoo, whistle, or other noise-maker to help identify your position to other players.

3. Never let anyone play through.

4. Concentrate on "feel."

5. "Hear" the ball into the cup.

CHAPTER 12

The Art of Telling Jokes When Your Opponent Is in the Bunker

JOKE-TELLING on the golf course is usually okay at the tee, while waiting for the foursome ahead of you, or while strolling with your fellow players toward your ball. To make money, though, you must break this general rule and tell jokes while your opponent attempts to extract himself from a hazard, or just after he has entered the hazard.

It is also important to laugh at your own jokes, especially when telling them to upset your opponent. A great laugher is the one about the flamenco dancer and the petroleum jelly. Excellent golf story.

CHAPTER 13

Proper Etiquette When You're Playing with a Complete Jerk

CERTAIN GOLFERS have the revolting habit of continually explaining the rules of the game and the proper etiquette for each and every situation, and of reviewing your swing for you after every stroke. These people average 103. They are Complete Jerks. When dealing with this kind of player, do this: deliver a nine-iron to the *solar plexus*, on about the third fairway. This is an extremely effective way to communicate your feelings concerning his advice, and it will preclude further critical or instructional comment.

CHAPTER **14**

Crying and How to Handle It

IT IS VERY DIFFICULT to maintain the proper attitude in the game of golf; to have a sense of humor. It is easy, once you are "hooked," to believe that you are better than you are; that the shanked four-iron was an aberration. Getting mad, while ugly and unpleasant for your partner, is easy to understand. Indeed, crying is perfectly reasonable.

But it doesn't help your game. Peter, a great athlete and a rational man, put this all in perspective. His friend Jeffrey was convinced that he was finally "getting" this game, so when, in the Eighth Bogey Four Open, Jeff sliced a drive into the water on the second hole, he was indignant, visibly agitated. He became extremely morose. He was crying.

As they left the tee, Peter walked with the tearful Jeffrey and asked him if he considered himself a good golfer. Jeffrey stammered, "Me? Naw, not really, well... of course not." And Peter simply asked: "Then what are you so pissed-off about?"

CHAPTER 15

How to Rationalize a Seven-Hour Round

I **PLAYED** with my boss once. He was patient and kind, even though the round took six hours. Over a beer after the round, as the sun was setting, he explained that his wife was "going to kill" him since he was supposed to pick up the kids at 4:00. He also said that if I didn't want to get fired, the next time I suggested a game of golf to him I should ask, "Would you like to play golf for about four hours?"

The way to rationalize long rounds like this, or golf in general, is always to be in a position to say it was "business." This works extremely well with wives and other superiors. (See Chapters 19 and 37.)

CHAPTER **16**

What to Do When You've Parred the Course by the Eleventh Hole

IT'S BEST never to realize that it's possible to "reach par," in the aggregate, after eleven holes. Many say that the only thing they regret about taking up the game so late in life is that they will never par a golf course. But it's merely a question of *when* you achieve par on a given course.

If you've reached par by the eleventh, it's best to adopt an attitude of serenity, to enjoy the physical beauty around you, and to focus on the peaceful tranquility of golf. (Read Chapters 14, 18, and 35 for further insights.) Then break the club across your knee.

How to Find a Ball that Everyone Else Saw Go in the Water

THIS IS is a tough one. Just deny it and use Drop Pockets to find your ball in the middle of the fairway. (See Chapter 10 again.)

When to Blame the Caddie

CADDIES can be blamed for almost everything.

For example:

1. The ball is lost because the caddie didn't watch it.

2. You shanked your three-iron because the caddie moved.

3. You overshot the green because the caddie chose the wrong club.

4. You missed the putt because the caddie read the green incorrectly.

5. You quit the game because your caddie suggested it.

CHAPTER 19

Why Your Wife No Longer Cares that You Birdied the Fourth
(or..."Frankly, Sweetie, I Don't Give a Damn")

THE DEGREE of indifference to success on the golf course varies widely from spouse to spouse, but basically she no longer cares because:

1. She's tired of hearing about it.

2. She knows you're lying anyway.

3. You play golf and ignore your primary responsibilities.

4. You've become a complete and utter fool.

5. She birdied it three times last week.

So if you birdie the fourth, don't mention it.

CHAPTER 20

How to Drive a Golf Cart When You're Two Down and Three to Go

IN THIS SITUATION, it is important to be the driver. That is, it has to be you behind the wheel, not your partner or opponent. You must therefore get to the cart first after you've made your fourth putt. If necessary, you must run, even though it is embarrassing, to beat the competition to the cart.

Having achieved this, the following are suggested:

1. Crash into the other carts. Always say, "God, I'm sorry, George. The pedal stuck."

2. Back into an opponent's cart. This usually will shake the bags loose as well, so you can unnerve an entire foursome this way.

3. Turn the key to "reverse" position—
   the buzzing noise is great—just before
   an opponent's putt or drive.

You will think of many more maneuvers,
like spin-outs, roll-outs, two-wheelers,
glide-stops, etc.

How to Let a Foursome Play Through Your Twosome Without Getting Embarrassed

THIS IS not possible. If you have to do this, don't play for two weeks. Then give up the game entirely. In shame.

The "Double-Hit" and When to Use It

ALSO KNOWN as the "Tee See Chin" maneuver, the double-hit can be a real aid in those situations when your first contact with the ball is poor. The double-hit is very difficult off the drive, but it can be easily accomplished with the wedge. The key is to make the secondary contact with the ball as soon as possible after you've realized how badly you've hit the ball in the first place. Otherwise your opponents will notice the maneuver and try to add strokes to your score, which is totally antithetical to the primary intent of the double-hit, which is to lower your score.

Be deft, and quick.

CHAPTER 23

How to Duck-Hook from the Bunker and Still Get Home in 10

YOU CAN DO THIS, really. It just takes proper attitude. Your mom tried to give you proper golf attitude, even though neither you nor she realized it, when she used to say: "Brush your teeth" and "Clean your room." If you had done these things in the first place, you probably wouldn't lie eight in the bunker.

So ask your mother.

CHAPTER **24**

The Insignificance of Proper Grip

THERE ARE many, many people who buy the "latest" woods, experimental irons, new-tech shoes, alloy equipment, and hydraulic lift bags at least once each season. They get their clubs re-gripped, cleaned, balanced, weighted, shortened, lengthened, beveled, polished, shined, and mono-grammed. They take lessons, do sit-ups, buy full-length mirrors, read books on technique, watch videos, and listen to cassettes in their sleep—all to acquire subliminal understanding of the perfect stroke. They take golf vacations and change their diets. They consult stress-management consultants, do yoga, run twenty miles a week, squeeze spring-loaded grips, and walk aerobically all the time.

Their pro told them what the proper grip was and how important it was, along, of course, with how to maintain a constant swing plane.

But you know it's a hoax. At your level, pal, just prac-tice as much as you can. Forget the grip. If you don't have it, face it: you're a terminal 90 and you'll never par a course.

CHAPTER **25**

Why You Should Always Leave the Course After Four Hours No Matter What Hole You're On

WHY PROLONG the agony? Leave, go home, chop wood, drink beer. Don't stay on the course. Doing so is bad, very bad, changes your relationship with your friends and colleagues, and causes minor memory loss. So just quietly stroll away, no matter what hole you're on, after four hours, max! You'll be glad you did it.

32 | HOW TO LINE UP YOUR FOURTH PUTT

The Myth of Proper Timing

ACTUALLY, this is no myth! Timing is everything, in every aspect of your life, forever. If you have it, you can hit 16 in regulation early in your career. Also, you can get rich in real estate. (See Chapters 4, 5, 12, 18, 24, 35, and 39.)

How to Enjoy Your Partner's 129

THIS IS one of the most difficult tasks in golf. First of all, if your partner is on his or her way to a 129, chances are that this poor soul is literally sick with embarrassment already, especially in view of the fact that everyone else in the foursome has probably ignored your partner completely for at least four holes. This person may even be crying, in which case, give him or her a copy of this book and point to Chapters 14 and 26. If things get real bad, direct him or her to Chapter 30 or employ the techniques outlined in Chapter 39.

In any event, enjoying someone else's mortification is difficult, but the best medicine is laughter. So, when your partner slices again on the tenth to penetrate the 60-stroke barrier a bit early, just laugh—hysterically. Ask the rest of the foursome, "Did you boys see that? Unbelievable!" See what happens. Hopefully your partner hasn't read Chapter 13.

CHAPTER 28

The Importance of Hysterical Laughter After the Banana Slice

IF THE BANANA SLICE is your partner's, this response will lead to a renewed relationship, an affirmation, hopefully, of trust and affection. If not, this will add at least a stroke to your opponent's game.

If the banana is yours, this response will divert the attention of the foursome from the actual location of your ball to a focus on how to make you stop laughing. You will thus be able to "find" your ball more easily, using Drop Pocket Slacks technology. (See Chapter 10.)

If the banana slice is your opponent's, he will spend the next twenty minutes trying to decide what to do to you, dropping at least five strokes in the process.

If the banana has been produced by your spouse ... do not, under any circumstances,

laugh. In fact, remain totally silent until your spouse decides to speak to you. Otherwise, awesome consequences will ensue. Awesome.

CHAPTER 29

How to Relax When You're Hitting "Five Off the Tee"

THERE'S A GUY named George. Now I know that George cannot possibly shoot under 100. Nevertheless, I saw George one day and he said, "Hey, Bobby, I shot an 85 yesterday." I said, "Sure, George." He said, "No, I mean it, I really was on!" So I said, "Then let's play tomorrow." George said, "Okay." You see, he had really convinced himself that he had shot an 85, and, long-term, such self-delusion is unhealthy, since it leads to broken thumbs and bad debts.

George slashed his way to the seventeenth, by which time, according to my card, he had accumulated 101 strokes (counting things like lost balls, out-of-bounds, and other events yielding additional strokes). I asked George what he had going into the last two holes, since I was considering an additional bet, having recorded 104 attempts at the ball myself. Stepping up to the tee, and very relaxed, George said: "I have 73 so far." I said, "Sure, George."

The seventeenth, par three, 190 yards, is "all carry," which means: do not top it, or hit it short, because there's nothing but water between tee and green. So George concentrated completely and hit a four-iron seventy-five yards, maximum elevation two feet, 45 degrees (on average) off-line, slice acceleration five feet per millisecond, one bounce on the water, and quickly thereafter to the bottom of the lake, far right. My stroke counter said George lay two.

George approached his bag, undaunted, still professional, silently concentrating, obviously having realized he'd neglected to compensate for the wind. He solemnly withdrew his three-iron from the bag and gently dropped his cigar near the back of the tee, preparing gravely for the next blow. The ball jumped two feet forward; the tee went into the water; a pound of turf spun out left. I felt that George lay four.

George took a confident puff on his cigar, and very slowly pulled out his driver. The ball sailed almost straight up, but on line, and, miraculously, three minutes later, came to rest forty-five feet from the pin, off the green, in the short rough.

George continued, and flubbed a chip. He three-putted: I sincerely thought that added up to "nine."

I said, "George, what did you get?" George said, "A five." I said, "Sure, George."

The whole time, George was totally relaxed. So the thing to learn here is, to relax when you're hitting five off the tee, you must ignore your real score. Don't start counting strokes until you successfully leave the tee with a good, strong shot.

Good, basic, moneymaking golf.

CHAPTER 30

How to Replace the Divots of Your Life

NO ONE has ever played the game of life without extracting a divot or two from the innocent and unsuspecting earth. Sometimes it's hard to repair these clumps of failure, the loamy mounds of major misses, particularly when poor shot selection and incompetent execution are continual problems in life for most of us, every single day.

There is a solution, thanks be to the Lord. Forget the debt; refuse the abuse. Ignore the hazards and bunkers of your job and responsibilities. Don't worry about the "daily divots" of existence.

Instead, consolidate! Adopt a single focus: PLAY GOLF and concentrate all your energy to answer the one important question: how to get home in five!

CHAPTER 31

The "Velcro Rip"— How to Gracefully Tear Open the Velcro Seal on Your Golf Glove

THERE'S NO graceful way to do this. But its value and effect far outweigh the obnoxious sound of its execution. The "Velcro Rip" is the best technique yet devised for doing in the opposition.

CHAPTER **32**

The Importance of Realizing that Most Golfers Are Bad Golfers

EVER PLAY Pebble Beach? The first time you do, if it's early in your career as a high-handicap golfer, you will be intimidated. This is because you think you will embarrass yourself on one of the world's great golf courses. Because you haven't yet realized that most golfers are bad golfers.

The day I shot 141 at Pebble Beach, there was a mixed foursome in front of us and a foursome from Japan behind. The Happy Couples took six hours to get around, and the boys from Tokyo never had a chance to play through: they took seven hours. See? They were all bad golfers, just like us, just like 99 percent of the people at Pebble Beach that day, like most people who play the game. Thank God.

CHAPTER 33

God and the Meaning of the Double Bogey

SIMPLE: The double bogey is a test of faith, developed by the Almighty as an efficient way to separate scratch believers from faithless hackers. If you can withstand a life of double bogeys, a special seat awaits you in the Golf Cart of Heaven. If you can come to understand the deeper meaning of the double bogey, you will reap great rewards. You will play the Final Nine with a smile on your face, knowing that a "Wider World of Sports" shall witness your penultimate putt—and shall forgive the Divots of Your Life!

Amen.

CHAPTER 34

How to Walk a 6,500-Yard Course in Less than 12,500 Yards

PLAY St. Andrews in Scotland—God's own natural golf course—Mecca. You will be thrilled to play where Henry VIII used to chip and putt.

One great caddie there is eighty-six years old. His name is Billy. I shot an eleven on the first hole and was obviously concerned, but Billy told me about Mr. Jeepers. Mr. Jeepers played the previous day and shot a forty-one on the first hole, and it got worse. At round's end, Jeepers asked Billy how caddies were paid at St. Andrews. Billy replied that he was paid by the round, but that he wished he were paid by the "'ardage." Mr. Jeepers asked why this was, and Billy said: "Because, laddie, today I've been on every goddamn square yard of this course!"

So if you're going to walk 12,500, ask for Billy. He'll ease your pain with comforting stories. He'll charge you by the yard, but if you use techniques set out here and in the final chapter, you'll win the Nassau no matter how far you walk.

CHAPTER 35

Profanity: Using It to Maximize Earnings on the Golf Course

PROFANITY is a natural inclination on the golf course, but its use must be goal-oriented. It is best to yell "Sheeeee...it" or its equivalent not after you have swung your club, the most natural thing, but just before your opponent swings his. About three to five times a round. This is usually good for at least seven strokes.

CHAPTER **36**

When to Play Dice Instead of Golf

WHEN YOUR handicap goes up two months in a row.

How Never to Pay for Another Golf Ball Again and Still Average 111

YOU NEVER PAY for golf balls, no matter how you play, if you are the chief financial officer of a large, publicly traded company. In this role, you play golf only "on business," and balls, dozens—with various logos—are handed to you before each round to induce you to buy goods and services from the generous giver.

So, try to become a CFO.

CHAPTER **38**

How to Feel Good About Yourself When Your Biggest Lifetime Drive Was 117

HOW COULD anyone feel good under such circumstances? If you can't do better than 117, you are in the wrong sport.

Take up piano.

CHAPTER **39**

When to Suggest Swing Corrections to Your Opponent

THE **TIMING** of Swing Correction Suggestions is obvious: whenever you're down by less than the number of holes left to play.

CHAPTER **40**

Why You Should Instruct Your Caddie to "Listen for the Ball" Off the Tee Rather than to "Watch the Ball"

IF YOUR HANDICAP is great (i.e., higher than 15), which means your game is not great, remind your caddie that he won't find your tee shot by watching it. He must locate it instead by listening for it. For it is not possible to see the ball on its first acute, smokeless burst into the atmosphere, because your ball never begins its journey in the direction, nor at the same angle or speed, as intended. NEVER.

So instruct your caddie to listen: for the thud into the hillock twenty yards out, for the crack into the tree ninety yards out, for the plunk into the water 115 yards out, for the yelp of the dog 121 yards out, for the screech of automobile tires 130 yards out, for the scream of the woman on the adjoining tee, ten yards back.

HOW TO LINE UP YOUR FOURTH PUTT | **51**

What to Do When the Divot Weighs 1.5 Pounds and Has Traveled Twenty-Five Yards, and Your Ball Has Not Moved

S END THE DIVOT to the National Institute for the Study of Unnatural Phenomena (STUNPH), donate the ball to your caddie, throw your clubs (bag and all) into the nearest water hazard, remove your glove, bury it in the nearest bunker, throw your shoes gently into the deep rough . . . then slowly, silently, leave the course forever.

How to Increase Your Opponent's Score When You Are Unable to Decrease Your Own

FIRST, read *How to Line Up Your Fourth Putt* over and over and over again to memorize Bobby Rusher's techniques, like the "Velcro Rip" for totally sabotaging your opponent's ability to perform. "Putt"—as it is affectionately known to readers the world over—is specifically designed to *increase* your opponent's score, not to lower your own. This masterwork of golf instruction is a brilliant compendium of the Techniques of Treachery in golf.

Next, buy Drop Pocket Golf Slacks™. (See Chapter 10.)

Finally, suggest to your opponent that you've compared his game to those of good golfers and have concluded that they (his game and the game of good golfers) have absolutely nothing in common.

CHAPTER 43

How to Play Your Second Shot from the Ladies' Tee Without Explaining Yourself in a Falsetto

As you must know by now, this is very difficult.

However, if you do hit your first shot in such a way that it is highly unlikely to reach the Ladies' Tee, it is best to yell, as soon as humanly possible after the initial contact with the ball, "Be the right club! Be the right club!" You quickly establish the theory that this ridiculous shot has nothing to do with your swing—it was simply a matter of inappropriate club selection.

As a consequence, your adversaries will begin to want to play faster, having concluded that you have lost your mind, or that you are indeed the jerk they hoped they would never have to play with again, or that you just don't have the focus to go beyond the Ladies' Tee. Your yelling "Be the right club!" in such situations is worth at least three strokes per round.

CHAPTER 44

How to Draw Your Divot from Left to Right: The Art of the Divot Draw

TO BECOME SKILLED at this particular shot, you have to realize that your irons are really in many ways uniquely designed garden tools. Speaking of which, it is sometimes helpful to refer to your partner as a "garden tool" when he or she actually accomplishes the Divot Draw. You would say, "Jim, you really are a garden tool," and see what happens next.

So, when delivering the clubhead to the ball, visualize the task as a form of violent weeding, in which your goal is to devastate the weed in one whack. One-whack weeding is fun, and the stroke, striking the club head sharply into the ground about two inches behind the ball, normally produces the Divot Draw or, occasionally, the Divot Fade.

Remember...One Whack. You are weeding. The weed must be removed and deposited elsewhere in one fell swoop of a five-iron. Practice, practice, practice, and you will be a regular Divot-Head yourself, in regulation, in no time at all.

CHAPTER 45

How to Hit a Ball on Your First Try

THIS IS difficult, but it can be done if you:

- Concentrate on hitting the ball on your first try.

- Keep the distance between your head and your feet constant at all times.

- Shift your weight, or lose some weight, or both, at the appropriate moment.

- Make sure to choose a club before you address the ball.

- Rotate through the lateral, conical, and spherical space that defines your relationship to the ball, both before and after any contact, expected or unexpected.

- Swing very slowly. It might not go far, but this could increase your chances.

- Absolutely maximize clubhead speed at point of expected impact.

If you manage to miss it on the first try, just yell "Be the right club" again. Your opponent will begin to consider having his ball retriever re-gripped.

CHAPTER 46

How to Hit a Ball on Your Second Try

IF YOU MISSED the ball on the first attempt, you must quickly convince all who watched you that it was a practice swing. If they protest, you *insist* that it was a practice swing. If they begin to ridicule you and to add strokes to your score, wait a few minutes, and, when no one is looking, loosen the straps holding your buddies' golf bags to their golf carts.

CHAPTER **47**

What to Do if You Find More Balls than You Lost

IF THIS occurs often, you are to be known as a "surplus" rather than a "deficit" player. You can develop into a supply-side golfer, and using Drop Pocket Slacks, you can help your partner out of almost any jam. Your deficits, as they apply to your golf game, are probably already legion, so concentrate on Surplus Golf.

Of course, you're going to need to re-grip your ball retriever to become a truly great surplus player, but it's worth it.

60 | HOW TO LINE UP YOUR FOURTH PUTT

CHAPTER 48

How to Manufacture a Good Lie in a Bad Situation

A good lie is really hard to find. But if you're in trouble—behind a tree, in a rut, suffering from Slipped Grip—try these:

- That's not my ball. I hit a Titleist. This is a Dunlop.

- Thank God for free drops!

- My caddie gave me the wrong club. I therefore get a free drop.

- I forgot! I gotta be home by three-thirty.

- This *never* happened when I was at my peak.

CHAPTER 49

How to Successfully Place the Ball on the Tee

FIRST, don't eat beans the night before a match.

Next, bend over. Insert the tee into the ground, leaving about 1.5 inches of tee visible above the ground. Adjust the tee a few times, stepping back each time to assess its perpendicularity. Go to the ball-washer and wash your ball, slowly and thoroughly. Dry it lovingly. Bend over again. Hover a bit above that little wooden spike you have labored so hard to position properly. Turn, still bent over, and grin at your opponents, and say, "the weather couldn't possibly be better, eh boys?" Then, slowly, deftly, gingerly place the ball on the top surface of the tee. Stand up, watch the tee seriously for a few seconds to be certain it is securely settled, then step back, pull out a cigar, and light up.

This is good for six strokes per round!

CHAPTER 50

What to Do if Your Partner Pulls Out a Felt-Tipped Pen When He Is Told that It Is His Turn to "Address" the Ball

WHEN THIS occurs, run to your cart and leave the premises as soon as possible. If you stay a moment longer, you will suffer symptoms of Terminal Slipped Grip, which include:

- A sense of disorientation and alienation.

- A feeling that you must address your partner in inappropriate ways.

- A desire to hurt your partner.

CHAPTER 51

When to Explain the Difference Between Red Stakes and Yellow Stakes

"S TAKE BAITING"** is the timely explanation to your opponent of the difference between the red stakes and the yellow stakes. This technique is similar to "snake-biting" in its effect on the opposition. You should explain the difference between red and yellow:

- When you're down two with three to go.

- Just after he touches the ground in a hazard bounded by stakes of any color.

CHAPTER 52

What to Do if You Hit the Ground Before You Hit the Ball

THIS DEPENDS on how long before you hit the ball you hit the ground. If you hit the ground long before you hit the ball, i.e., if the time span is more than ten seconds, you have just executed a "practice swing." If the time span is between five and ten seconds, you say, "Damn, this is a hard course!" If the delay is less than five seconds, the other members of your foursome will say you have "flubbed" the ball, or, less politely, "hit a hideous shot," to which you reply, "Stick it, Divot-Brain."

What to Do if You Hit the Ground Well, Before You Hit the Ball

THIS could indicate that your game is gardening, not golf. Try again. If it happens again, throw your clubs away and go stencil the driveway.

How to Behave if You Hit the Ground Well, and Do Not Hit the Ball at All

JUST announce that your intention was indeed to hit the ground well, that you were overcome with a desire to do so—hit the ground well—but that it is something that you have difficulty explaining. That it happens to you from time to time. That you find it deeply satisfying. That you quit.

How to React if You Simply Just Hit the Ground

YOU MEAN, if *you* hit the ground? Or do you mean if you hit the ground with your club? This is getting ridiculous.

What to Do if Your Partner Hits the Dirt

IF THIS HAPPENS more than every once in a while, and you still play with the same partner regularly, do nothing, and say nothing (other than, "Get up, stupid. You're not hurt.") You have a rare and patient partner. If this happens a lot, get a new caddie. If your partner hits the dirt when you swing, and he doesn't get up, hit the dirt yourself.

CHAPTER 57

How to Invoke the Law of Gravity to Modify Your Score

"A BALL which rolls directly over the cup without dropping in is deemed to have dropped in." This is the ancient and universal law of gravity, which obviously supersedes the merely mortal rules of golf. There are many situations in golf where the law of gravity can be used to lower your score. For example:

- When you drop your club onto the floor of your golf cart as your opponent attempts to sink his fourth putt. This was due to your inability to control the force of gravity on your club. Just say "Sorry, I have made a grave error."

- When you drop your beer can onto the cart path just prior to your opponent's realization that, because of this, he has flubbed a three-iron.

What to Do if Your Opponent Says, "You Could Blow This" Just Before You Attempt to Execute a Short Fourth Putt

BLOW THE BALL IN, read *How to Line Up Your Fourth Putt* one more time, and hurl your ball retriever directly at your advisor.

How to Estimate the Distance the Ball Would Have Traveled Were It Not Unjustly Interrupted on Its Way to Where It Was Supposedly Going

INVOKE the law of gravity, using, as a measuring standard, half the length of your ball retriever, plus three times the actual distance, multiplied by the number of free drops taken in the last four holes. Then place your ball wherever you think it is most helpful.

CHAPTER 60

When to Explain the Difference Between a Lost Ball and a Stolen Ball

BASICALLY, there is no such thing as a lost ball, i.e., a ball is not lost if the ball said to be lost is or was yours. You know the ball is somewhere on the course and will eventually be found by someone, who, it is sad to report, will probably not return the ball to you. This is a tragedy of human nature, but such a ball is therefore stolen (or is to be considered as effectively or constructively stolen) and consequently no strokes should ever be added to your card in such situations.

It is very helpful to highlight this rule for your opponents when you lose (temporarily misplace) your ball. If your opposition misplaces a ball, it is a lost ball for sure. Two-stroke penalty. Maybe three.

CHAPTER 61

When to Call Someone a "Sprinkler Head"

IF YOU REFER to your opponent as a "Sprinkler Head" at the appropriate moment, such as just after he begins a downswing, you will increase his score, definitely. He might respond with "You are a Dingbat Wedge-nosed Dork," which could be the beginning of an unforgettable round.

CHAPTER 62

How to Claim Your Company-Logo Balls in the Used-Ball Basket in the Pro Shop

IF YOU FIND your company logo balls in the basket, you can say a number of things:

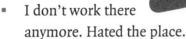

- Gosh! George has been losing a lot of balls.

- I don't work there anymore. Hated the place.

- Hey, those are mine!

- How could you possibly sleep at night after putting a red stripe on my balls?!

CHAPTER 63

How to Handle "Sprinkler-Head Panic"

SPRINKLER-HEAD PANIC is a natural phenomenon on the course. Use it to your advantage:

- Get to know the watering timetable. Approach the sixth when the fairways are being watered. Position your opponent appropriately.

- Befriend the greenskeeper. Pay him well to start the sprinklers when you give the signal.

Body Blocks and When to Use Them

USE THESE TOOLS when you're two down and three to go.

When to Use the Unsolicited Bear Hug in Lieu of the Devious Drop

GOLF IS A GAME of contentment, quiet resolve, little chatter, intense concentration, and long hours of uninterrupted walking and standing, standing and walking, with an occasional swing of the club (107 is the worldwide average number of such swings for eighteen holes).

Noisy the game of golf is not supposed to be! Congratulatory bear hugs after a birdie putt? NO! A big wet one on the cheek of your opponent when he hits a good long iron? God, no!

On the other hand, why not?

What to Do When Your Average Number of Hits Is Less than One-Fifth Your Average Number of Actual Swings

YOU HAVE an obvious problem: you are taking too many practice swings. (See Chapter 46.) It is also very possible that you should give up the game very, very soon.

How to Converse with a Friend Who Claims He Got "Closest to the Pin" on a Par-Three Contest

GEORGE: Hey, Bobby, I got closest to the pin on the fourth today!

BOBBY: How many strokes did it take you?

GEORGE: Very funny. It was a par three, dingbat. A hundred and twenty-seven yards, par three. It was my tee shot, fool.

BOBBY: Okay, okay, George. Relax. Sorreee. Don't be so sensitive. What club did you use?

GEORGE: I used a four-wood, if you don't mind.

BOBBY: A four wood!? You could hurt yourself.

GEORGE: Listen, divot-head, take a hike!

BOBBY: Okay, sprinkler-brain.

GEORGE: Bunker-butt, shank-lips.

BOBBY: Sit on it, wedge-face, lard-ass, four-wood-for-brains.

GEORGE: I'm never going to play with you again.

BOBBY: Relax, George. Relax.

CHAPTER 68

When to Discuss Waggling and Wobbling with Your Opponent

TO ERR is human; to wobble is unforgivable. When your opponent is waggling, say that he or she is wobbling. After the look you receive, you can proceed to mention additional ways to describe your opponent:

Waggler, wilter, wiggler, lunger, waiverer, waverer, bumbler, fumbler, groper, waffler, staggerer, lurcher, lunger, stabber, rammer, thruster, plunger, teeterer, totterer, staggerer, strayer, tumbler, tripper, hoverer, drooper, sagger, shriveler, witherer.

Swing slowerer.

CHAPTER **69**

What to Do When You Splash into the Water

"You mean his ball went into the water?"

"No. He went into the water. He was trying to 'collapse' through the ball, a new technique he learned that morning from reading the classic, *Vardon on Water*, but he collapsed too thoroughly and missed the ball entirely. The momentum of this attempt at making contact with the ball brought his entire body much too far left. He wobbled for a bit, lurched left-ward in a failed attempt to adjust his balance to the right. He hovered. He was dazed and startled, like a deer caught in the headlights of his golf cart. He tried to speak. He meant desperately to regain his balance and explain himself."

"He went into the lake. He 'splashed.' Understand? Never laughed so hard in my life. Of course he had no sense of humor whatsoever. He climbed up out of the water, skinning his knee on the rocks, grabbed his wedge and threw it at me! He takes the game entirely too seriously. Can you believe that?"

CHAPTER **70**

What Exactly Is a Bunker-Burp and Exactly What Should You Do About It

A BUNKER-BURP is related to a Chili-Dip, a stroke known to all golfers, only worse.

CHAPTER 71

How to Play with a Hangover

SOME PEOPLE SAY that a hangover smoothes out the swing. Because your body is so relaxed. Some folks have been known to play in the morning still asphyxiated.

If you still have a hangover (which includes throbbing cranial pain, blurred vision, itching teeth, red eyes, shaky hands, wobbly legs, pale visage), get up at least four hours before your tee time. For a 7:30 A.M. tee-time, you must get up at 3:30 A.M. Carefully observe yourself in the mirror and say one or both of the following prayers:

1. Lord, please help me get through this one and I promise I'll get through the next one myself.

2. Lord, please, if you ever give me a new body, be sure to give me a brain to go along with it.

CHAPTER 72

The Importance of Realizing that a Gimme Is Any Shot After Your Tenth

YOU WILL *never* grant gimmes to your opponent if you have read *How to Line Up Your Fourth Putt*. If, for example, your adversary has an eighteen-inch putt for bogey on the fourth and he asks "gimme?" you say "no way, Bunker-butt. I'm afraid you'll have to sink that putt." Ninety-five percent of the time, two things happen:

A. He begins to fume and shake and misses the putt, and

B. He also pushes his drive on the next tee into the woods.

It is important, however, to announce that your partner's eighteen-inch putt is good. You say, "That's good." Your opponents, if you have already referred to them as Bunker-butts, will deny the gimme. You then argue with them, observing, "This is just a game for Pete's sake." They will respond with "Sorry, the rules are the rules." You then say "Okay, Sprinkler-head." They then begin to fume and shake and miss their putts.

CHAPTER 73

Why You Should Never Purchase "Extra Long" Balls

"**E**XTRA LONG" balls, when well hit, always go deeper into the woods than regular golf balls do. When they are poorly hit, especially on the first try, or when they are well hit backwards, such balls leave you subject to lawsuits and other violence. George once hit an Extra Long backwards on his first try, slamming his boss's wife in the forearm and whacking the boss himself on the forehead. George got no severance and is still looking for work, although it has occurred to co-workers that he certainly won some kind of contest.

CHAPTER 74

When to Pick Up a Lost Ball Before It Stops Rolling

IF YOU CAN do this, you are deft and quick indeed. If the lost ball comes from another foursome, pocket it quickly if you value your life. (Check the logo carefully, for obvious reasons.) If the ball is your partner's, set it gently atop a small grassy prominence and yell, "Found it!"

CHAPTER 75

How to Reach a Hazard in One Shot

1. Determine the distance to the hazard by estimating where you should have been in the first place.

2. Calculate the dimensions of the hazard you are trying to reach. How far to the near edge? What is the distance to the far edge, to the lateral entry points, from where you are, or where you could have been, if your shank were more powerful?

3. Choose the club that maximizes the probability that you will *miss* the hazard. (Choosing the club you *think* will put you in the hazard is a bad decision indeed, for obvious reasons.)

4. For show, check the wind with a moistened forefinger.

5. For show, stand next to your bag with your caddie. Quietly ask him how he is doing these days, but staring into

the distance, as if you knew what you were doing.

6. Pull out the club you have identified as appropriate to the task of missing the hazard.

7. Step up and take a swing.

8. If you actually hit the ball on your first try, it will definitely go right into the hazard.

CHAPTER 76

When You Should Keep Your Putts Low

YOU SHOULD TRY to keep your putts low if you fear that your trajectory on short putts has been excessive. Try to explain your dilemma at your next lesson by telling the pro that your putts are coming in a little hot and a little high. Let the author know what he says.

CHAPTER **77**

If You Have a Stroke in the Middle of Your Stroke

IN A SENSE, if you have no stroke to begin with, it is unlikely that you will have a stroke at any time whatsoever after the beginning. However, there is a remote possibility here, so be sure to begin your stroke after you have achieved the middle of the initial stroke, thereby minimizing the likelihood of a stroke in the middle. You should always play with a paramedic anyway if your handicap is above 29.

When You Should Hand a Compass to Your Opponent

THE BEST TIME to do this is on the green, after you have explained in detail to your opponent exactly how he should line up his fourth putt. Just hand him the compass and say, "If you miss your fourth putt, this will help you find your way home."

Why It Doesn't Matter if the Dog Leg's Left or the Dog Leg's Right

IF YOU THINK it doesn't matter, it is time to re-grip your ball retriever. If the dog leg's left, you need, if you are right-handed, to swing as hard as you possibly can. If the dog leg's right, and you are left-handed, you need to learn how to hit a Titleist 3 from the rough when you teed off with a Dunlop 2.

When to Perform the Heimlich Maneuver on Your Opponent

WHENEVER he or she is more than one hole ahead of you on the back nine, or more than two holes ahead of you on the front.

When to Invoke the Same-Day Rule

THIS TECHNIQUE is an excellent money-maker, and it is particularly helpful when utilized against slower players who are beating you badly. It's the equivalent, more or less, of successfully distracting a pitcher and bringing about a balk.

Let's say you're down two with three to go, and your opponents have been driving you nuts the entire round because of their ridiculously slow pace of play. You can produce the near-equivalent of a balk—a shank, a flub, a Chili-Dip, a whiff, or a stub—in many ways:

1. Yelling at the right moment. This is no good, though, because you will be accused of poor etiquette, or of being a "Complete Jerk." (See Chapter 13.)

2. Use the "Velcro Rip." (See Chapter 31.) You could get hurt, though.

3. You could suggest swing corrections at the proper moment, but, by the six-

teenth hole, you will probably have done this four or five times already.

4. You could say, "It's too dark"—but it may be noon.

NO! Now is the time for you to explain the "Same-Day Rule." After your opponent has lined up his shot, completed his waggle, and is just about to begin his backswing, you say, "Uh, Sam, you know, we *are* playing the Same-Day Rule." Sam will turn and glare at you, the way your wife does when you say you're going to go play golf. Be strong and say, "Sorry, Sam, but, my goodness, if you took any more time between shots we'd be here all week." He will probably throw his club at you. Just duck. Then apologize again, saying, "I was just trying to help."

Congratulations. Sam will execute a textbook shank on the next shot, and you will be only one down with two to go. Use this technique again on the very next hole!

CHAPTER 82

What to Do When You Reach a Par-Three and Your Partner Complains that He Can't Find His Big Bertha

THIS HAPPENS much too often, especially when playing with an idiot. The first time this happens, you gently admonish him for his poor choice of clubs. The second time it happens, you insist that he put the club back into the bag and let you choose his clubs for him. If he does this a third time, it is the proper moment to announce that you think you are playing with a "Complete Jerk" (see Chapter 13), that you are leaving the course, and that you refuse to play with this person ever again.

CHAPTER 83

Final Chapter:
How to Choose
a Caddie

THIS DECISION can be very important.
Here's how to interview a prospective caddie:

YOU WHISPER:	HE REPLIES:
"I only have one ball in my bag today."	"I understand completely, sir. I have some extra balls in my pants."
"Are you wearing Drop Pocket Golf Slacks?"	"Yes, sir."
"Buy 'em in Miami?"	"Yes, sir."
"Can you see well over long distances?"	"I have always found the ball hit by the person whose bag is across my shoulder, sir."
"Do you know that it is possible to have a good lie, even when you're in the woods?"	"I don't, sir. But I appreciate your predicament."
"How much is six plus seven plus five?	"Twelve, sir."
"Do you have change for a fifty-dollar bill?"	"I don't, sir. But I appreciate your predicament."
"Will you caddie for me today?"	"Of course, sir."

See?

Religious Responses to Missing A Fourth Putt

TAOISM: This stuff happens.

CONFUCIANISM: Confucius say: "This stuff happens."

BUDDHISM: This stuff will happen again.

HINDUISM: This has all happened before.

ZEN: What is the sound of this stuff happening?

ISLAM: When this sort of thing happens, it is the will of Allah.

JUDAISM: Why does this sort of thing always happen to me?

CATHOLICISM: If this is happening, I must deserve it.

PROTESTANTISM: Let these things happen to someone else.

ATHEISM: I can't believe this stuff is happening.

I, myself, a Reform Druid, in my case, when stuff like this happens, I ignore it.

Two Poems

I Shank

I SHANK, WHILE HE HITS TRUE AND
HIGH
THERE, BUT FOR THE GOD OF GRACE,
GO I.

Thoughts on the Dew Delay

WHAT SHOULD ONE DO

WHEN LOST IN THE DOO DOO

IN THE MORNING DEW?

A DOO DOO DEW DELAY

CAN WASH YOUR SCORE AWAY.

The Dot System of Scoring

THE DOT SYSTEM of measuring performance on the golf course is really a form of modified Stableford scoring. It is actually the only way that match competition should be scored in tournaments involving players with handicaps of 22 or more.

Basically, the system properly rewards the "highly handicapped" player whenever he is able to do anything correctly on the golf course, which is rarely. It minimizes psychological depression, since even a round of triple bogeys might yield a dot or two.

To clarify: this system, which applauds you if you can manage to do anything right, gives you a "dot" for certain events, as follows. (You know what a "dot" is: a tiny circular mark on the card, made by stubbing the pencil directly at the card, point first, with a sharp, downward, vertical motion. Like a sand shot. Understand?)

Unsuccessfully teeing the ball: . . . .- 3 dots

Teeing the ball without it
falling off the tee: . . . .+ 11 dots

Hitting the ball on the first try: . . . .+ 2 dots

Hitting the ball on the second try: . . . .+ 5 dots

Wearing color-coordinated
slacks and shirt: . . . .+ 3 dots

Wearing plaid slacks: . . . .- 8 dots

Wearing rubber golf shoes: . . . .- 5 dots

Wearing a baggy Hawaiian shirt: . . . . . .- 8 dots

Keeping your shirt tucked in: . . . .+ 10 dots

Wearing Drop Pocket
Golf Pants: . . . .+ 15 dots

Slicing into the water: . . . .- 10 dots

Hitting straight into the water: . . . .+ 6 dots

Hitting straight: . . . .+ 2 dots

Hitting the fairway in
the air off the tee: . . . .+ 7 dots

Staying on the fairway off the tee: . . . . .+ 1 dot

Choosing the right club: . . . .+ 2 dots

Choosing the wrong club: . . . .- 1 dot

Staying out of the bunkers
on a given hole: . . . .+ 3 dots

Getting out of a bunker
in less than three strokes: . . . .+ 6 dots

Par: . . . . + 8 dots
(6 dots if done "in regulation")

Birdie: . . . .+ 10 dots

Eagle: . . . .+ 11 dots

Sandy: . . . .+ 12 dots

Wedgy: . . . .+ 13 dots

One-putting a green: . . . .+ 7 dots

Chipping in: . . . .+ 13 dots

Sinking your fourth putt: . . . .+ 25 dots

Reaching the green in regulation: . . . . .+ 6 dots

Bogey: . . . .+ 4 dots

Double Bogey: . . . .+ 3 dots

Triple Bogey: . . . .+ 2 dots

Reaching the green on your second
shot on a par-three: . . . .+ 7 dots

Picking up the wrong ball:
- if it's an opponent's . . . .+ 4 dots
- if it's your partner's . . . .- 10 dots

Hitting the wrong ball
(if you hit it well): . . . .+ 6 dots

Finding more balls than you've lost: . . .+ 9 dots

So, let's say your first hole of the day is a par-five, 510 yards. The following chart illustrates a possible Dot System scoring result, assuming a certain performance against an opponent, and simultaneously tallies the actual number of strokes:

YOU	OPPONENT	YOU		OPPONENT	
		DOTS EARNED	CUM STROKES	DOTS EARNED	CUM STROKES
1 You're wearing "Drop Pocket Golf Slacks."	He's wearing plaid slacks.	+15	0	-8	0
2 Your shirt is tucked in.	He's wearing a baggy Hawaiian shirt.	+10	0	-8	0
3 You're wearing brand new leather golf shoes.	He's wearing rubber golf shoes.	0	0	-5	0
4 You do the "Velcro Rip."	His ball falls off during tee-up.	0	0	-3	0
5 You say, "Sorry."	He says, "No problem."	0	0	0	0
6 You clean your ball, loudly.	He slices his drive into the water.	0	0	-10	2
7 You successfully tee-up.	He is not smiling.	+11	0	0	2
8 You miss your first attempt completely.	He is smiling.	0	1	0	2
9 You slice your second attempt onto the fairway, 117 yards out.	He smiles and says, "That'll work."	+13	3	0	2
10 You smile.	He hits his second attempt 220 yards, hits rough first, ends up in the fairway.	0	3	+1	3

	YOU	OPPONENT	YOU		OPPONENT	
			DOTS EARNED	CUM STROKES	DOTS EARNED	CUM STROKES
11	You hook your fourth shot into the left rough.	He says, "You'll be alright."	0	4	0	3
12	You put your cart in reverse and the buzzer sounds.	He shanks a 3- iron into a tree.	0	4	0	4
13	You say, "You've still got a line on it."	He intends to kill you.	0	4	0	4
14	You smile.	He hits a 5-wood safely forward, straight.	0	4	+2	5
15	You hit a career 3-iron into the green, straight, and lie 3 feet from the hole.	He is totally stunned.	+2	5	0	5
16	You say, "I've never done that before!"	He says, "Bullshit!"	0	5	0	5
17	You are laughing hysterically.	He has just banana-sliced into the trap.	0	5	0	6
18	You say, "Sorry."	He just looks at you.	0	5	0	6
19	You mark your ball.	He just looks at you.	0	5	0	6
20	You say "Hello" loudly, to a friend in a passing foursome.	He flubs his trap shot and throws his wedge at you.	0	5	0	7

	YOU	OPPONENT			
YOU	**OPPONENT**	**DOTS EARNED**	**CUM STROKES**	**DOTS EARNED**	**CUM STROKES**
21 You say, "Hey, it's only a game for Christsake!"	He just looks at you.	0	5	0	7
22 You smile.	He gets out of the trap to the green.	0	5	+6	8
23 You smile.	He putts two.	0	5	0	10
24 You putt three times.	He says, "Tough green, eh?"	0	8	0	10
25 You <u>Line Up Your Fourth Putt</u>, and sink it.	He slowly grabs his wedge, like a baseball bat, and just looks at you, red with rage.	+25	9	0	10
26 You say "I'm one up."	He throws his bag into the water, his shoes into the rough, his gloves into the bunker, and leaves the course forever.	0	9	0	10
TOTALS		**+76**	**9**	**-25**	**10**

The Descending Blow

In learning how to be a pro,
A basic stroke is the descending blow.

Cannot be forced through fallen snow,
Nor deep beneath the river's flow.

So if in trying you stub your toe,
Just execute the forward throw!

R. Paul (Bobby) Rusher lives quietly with his obedient wife (see Chapter 19) and two lovely children in Budapest, where he is currently focusing his energies on securing the video rights for *Putt, The Musical*.

He has been, and continues to be, deeply involved in Swedish Auto Repair, Insurance Policy Wording Analysis, and development of this book's sequel, *When to Re-grip Your Ball Retriever.*©

OK?